Rhythm Definition 101 Quarter Note Rhythms, Examples, Exercises and Patterns

Taura Eruera

Rhythm Definition 101 Quarter Note Rhythms, Examples, Exercises and Patterns

Published by Hookmedia Co Ltd

Hookmedia Co Ltd

© Copyright Taura Eruera 2012. All Rights Reserved.

Email: hookmediapublications@gmail.com

National Library of New Zealand

ISBN 978-1-877321-05-4
Kindle ISBN 978-1-877321-06-1

Rhythm Definition Series

Rhythm Definition 101   Quarter Note
Rhythms, Examples, Exercises and Patterns
Rhythm Definition 102   Eighth Note
Rhythms, Examples, Exercises and Patterns
Rhythm Definition 103   Sixteenth Note
Rhythms, Examples, Exercises and Patterns
Rhythm Definition 104   Triplet Eighth Note
Rhythms, Examples, Exercises and Patterns
Rhythm Definition 105   Syncopated Triplet Eighth Note
Rhythms, Examples, Exercises and Patterns
Rhythm Definition 106   Quarter Note
Rhythms, Examples, Exercises and Patterns
Rhythm Definition 107   Eighth Note
Rhythms, Examples, Exercises and Patterns
Rhythm Definition 201   Quarter Note
Rhythms, Examples, Exercises and Patterns
Rhythm Definition 202   Eighth Note
Rhythms, Examples, Exercises and Patterns
Rhythm Definition 203   Sixteenth Note
Rhythms, Examples, Exercises and Patterns

"When you think about those guys like BB King who can do solos with two or three notes: they've only got two or three notes! What could it be that they are utilising to make their solo's great? The rhythm! That's all they've got! The really big deal is to remember that it's all about rhythm."

Justin Sandercoe

It's all about Rhythm

https://youtu.be/AgR2ppyichs

For Joe, George, Michael, John H, John V.K., Hugh, Rosie, James, Sam B, Emma, Nick, Lance, Tyler and Samuel: awesome Dobodobo rhythm and guitar students.

Table of Contents

Welcome   1
Comparison with Rhythm Book 101........................ 8
Suggestions for using this book....................... 8
About Rhythmisation Levels............................ 9

Rhythmisation Pronunciation Guide......................... 11
   Vowel Pronunciation................................. 11
   Vowel Length.. 11
   Dobodobo Vocabulary Vowel Lengths................... 11
   Table of One Bar Rhythmisation Levels............... 12
   Table of Two Bar Rhythmisation Levels............... 12
   Rhythm Definition 101 Quarter Note Rhythmisations
   Vocabulary.. 13

EIGHT ATTACK RHYTHMS....................................... 17
   8 Attack Rhythms 4+4................................ 17

SEVEN ATTACK RHYTHMS....................................... 19
   7 Attack Rhythms 4+3 CV............................. 19
   7 Attack Rhythms 3+4 VC............................. 19

SIX ATTACK RHYTHMS... 21
   6 Attack Rhythms 4+2 CV............................. 21
   6 Attack Rhythms 3+3 CV............................. 21
   6 Attack Rhythms 3+3 VC............................. 23
   6 Attack Rhythms 2+4 VC............................. 25

FIVE ATTACK RHYTHMS.. 27
   5 Attack Rhythms 4+1................................ 27
   5 Attack Rhythms 3+2 VC............................. 27
   5 Attack Rhythms 2+3 CV............................. 30
   5 Attack Rhythms 1+4................................ 33

```
FOUR ATTACK RHYTHMS............................................. 35
    4 Attack Rhythms 4+0....................................... 35
    4 Attack Rhythms 2+2 CV.................................... 36
    4 Attack Rhythms 2+2 VC.................................... 41
    4 Attack Rhythms 1+3 VC.................................... 46

THREE ATTACK RHYTHMS............................................ 49
    3 Attack Rhythms 3+0 VC.................................... 49
    3 Attack Rhythms 2+1 VC.................................... 49
    3 Attack Rhythms 1+2 CV.................................... 51
    3 Attack Rhythms 0+3 CV.................................... 53

TWO ATTACK RHYTHMS.............................................. 55
    2 Attack Rhythms 2+0 VC.................................... 55
    2 Attack Rhythms 1+1 CV.................................... 55
    2 Attack Rhythms 1+1 VC.................................... 56
    2 Attack Rhythms 0+2 CV.................................... 57

ONE ATTACK RHYTHMS.............................................. 59
    1 Attack Rhythms 1+0 VC.................................... 59
    1 Attack Rhythms 0+1....................................... 59

NO ATTACK RHYTHMS............................................... 59
    0 Attack Rhythms 0+0....................................... 59

Congratulations................................................. 61
    Where to next?............................................. 62

Appendices ....................................................... I
    How Long To Read This Book .............................. III

About the Author ................................................. V
    Join Rhythmisation Insights............................. VII
    Learn more about Rythmisation.......................... VIII
```

Welcome

Welcome to Rhythm Definition 101 Quarter Note Rhythms Examples, Exercises and Patterns.

If you have come here after reading Rhythm Book 101 Quarter Note Rhythm Patterns, you are in the right place. If you haven't yet read Rhythm Book 101, reading it before you start this book is a good idea. This book presumes that you have done so and that you are familiar with all the Book 101 concepts of rhythmisation. They won't be repeated here.

The purpose of this book is to teach you the rhythmisation definitions of quarter note rhythms that make up the dobodobo quarter note vocabulary.

The quarter note beat provides the basic pulse of western music. It is the underlying rhythm level of many popular musical styles.

It is the reference rhythm level that can be expanded by being doubled in length (to a half note) or quadrupled (to a whole note). The quarter note can also be divided (into eighth notes) or subdivided (into sixteenth notes).

Having a command of the quarter note *seed* rhythm and its *derivational* rhythms is a mandatory pre-requisite to comprehending and playing all five rhythm levels, whether employed in duple, triple or other tuple meters (like 2/4, 3/4, 5/4, 7/4 and so on).

Continuing this journey of internalising the quarter note definitions is the focus of this book.

According to the Google Keyword Tool, the most searched rhythm study phrase is rhythm definition, followed by define rhythm and definition of rhythm.

This is a timely reminder about how important a useful working definition of rhythm actually is for the musician, whether a beginner or seasoned professional.

It is also a reminder about how the concept of rhythm is a bit like the concept of culture. Everybody knows all about it until they have to explain it to, or define it for, themselves or somebody else.

We are reminded too that Rhythmisation is actually a rhythm definition system that uniquely defines each and every rhythm: from the most global to the most forensic level.

Rhythmisation defines rhythm levels, rhythm vocabularies, rhythm phrases (of any length), rhythm words and rhythm syllables.

In this volume you will experience the rhythmisation definition of the quarter note seed rhythm, (defined as dobodobo) and the twenty four, derived dobodobo, quarter note, rhythms. These twenty-four rhythms are individually, and uniquely, defined.

You will learn these twenty-five definitions as rhythm words and converse with this vocabulary across fourteen hundred and ninety-eight bars.

Even more, you will learn these rhythm definition words through **text only**: with no recourse whatsoever to notation.

Perhaps the more accurate word to use here is review rather than learn.

I am expecting that you have already experienced the sixteen word vocabulary, and the seven hundred and fifty-eight bars of dobodobo rhythms, in Rhythm Book 101 Quarter Note Rhythm Patterns. In this case you are not learning these dobodobo concepts for the first time. You are *reviewing* them.

There are *three* main differences between Rhythm Book 101 and this Rhythm Definition 101 book. This book differs in that it:

- is text-only: it is completely notation-free
- has a twenty five rhythm vocabulary (rather than sixteen)
- offers fourteen hundred and ninety-eight bars of conversation (rather than seven hundred and fifty-eight)

Any musician schooled in notation would look at the text and wonder, "how on earth can English text effectively convey rhythm meaning?"

Any graduate of Rhythm Book 101 would know that the English vowels -- e, u, o, a, i --can correctly express rhythm duration and that the b, d and s consonants can express rhythmic position, on both the surface rhythm level and on the underlying level of rhythm alternation.

What Rhythm Book 101 offered was an introduction to rhythm with notation *and* rhythmisation presented side by side.

What Rhythm Definition 101 offers in contrast, is the opportunity to experience rhythm definition and instruction, strictly, in the verbal and text realm.

This focus requires you, the reader, to focus on talking rhythm, talking rhythmisation, talking rhythm duration at will, without the demand of notation being present: peripherally or primarily.

This volume offers you the opportunity to firmly embed the twenty-five dobodobo rhythms in three important places:

1. your mind;
2. your ear;
3. your speech.

In simple terms you are developing a dobodobo-sensitive brain, a dobodobo-sensitive ear and dobodobo-sensitive speech. From the point of view of your whole musical body, your outcome from this volume is a dobodobo **head**.

This is no trivial achievement. If your rhythm definitions are not in your head, no other part of the body will be able to receive rhythm instructions or execute rhythms on demand for you.

(In Rhythm Guitar 101 Quarter Note Strumming Patterns, you extend this dobodobo-sensitive head capability to a dobodobo-sensitive strumming arm and dubudubu-sensitive tempo feet capability.)

At the end of this book you will:

- talk a twenty-five rhythm dobodobo vocabulary with a metronome,
- talk fourteen hundred and ninety-eight bars of essential quarter note rhythms,
- write out twenty-five dobodobo rhythms in text or simple English.

There are also two hidden benefits that may reveal themselves to you by the end of the book.

The first hidden benefit is the ability to tab out any dobodobo rhythm you want. How?

If you are an electric bass player, for example, you can write out a dobodobo rhythm in rhythmisation. Like this:

    do da bo ba da bo ba~o da ba bu

Then you can write out bass guitar tab above the rhythmisation. Then tab a melody like this:

```
E:|-----2-------2-----------4---2-------------------
D:|----------------2---4----------------------------
A:|----------------------------------2--------------
E:|---------0-----------------------------4---0-----
      do  da  bo  ba  da  bo  ba~o  da  ba  bu
```

Now, you have the rhythm, the pitches and the pitch locations all written out.

I'm sure that guitar, mandolin, banjo, lute and other fretted (and unfretted) instrument players can see how this applies to their instrument.

The second hidden benefit is the ability to transcribe any dobodobo melody you hear.

For example, here is a melodic rhythm that just about every native English speaker will know; and will be able to transcribe by the end of this book. Let's imagine you have sung this melody and transcribed the rhythmisation as follows:

    dobo dobo dobo doso | dobo dobo dobo doso |
    dobo dobo dobo doso | dobo dobo dobo doso |
    dobo dobo dobo doso | dobo dobo dobo doso |

Now that you have transcribed the rhythm, tabbing the melody notes is just a matter of writing each fret location on the string above each rhythm syllable. (Notice the rhythmisation is spaced out to make the tab clear. Note there is no note for so because so is a rest.) Continuing with our hypothetical bass player, you get this result.

```
G:|------------------------------------------------------------
D:|------0--0--7--7--9--9--7--------5--5—-4--4--2--2--0-----
A:|------------------------------------------------------------
E:|------------------------------------------------------------
        Do bo do bo do bo do so | do bo do bo do bo do so |


G:|------------------------------------------------------------
D:|-----7--7--5--5—-4--4--2--------7--7--5--5—-4--4---2-----
A:|------------------------------------------------------------
E:|------------------------------------------------------------
        Do bo do bo do bo do so | do bo do bo do bo do so |
```

```
G:|------------------------------------------------------
D:|-----0--0--7--7--9--9--7-------5--5--4--4--2--2--0------
A:|------------------------------------------------------
E:|------------------------------------------------------
      Do bo do bo do bo do so | do bo do bo do bo do so
```

In this example you *heard* a melody, *transcribed* the rhythm, *discovered* the melody notes on your instrument and *tabbed* them. You have just completed the key steps of successful transcription. This powerful benefit is yours by the end of this book.

Meanwhile, here you are, right at the beginning.

When you talk this book at a metronome speed of MM60, you'll spend only one hour and forty minutes talking these fourteen hundred and ninety-eight bars. By the time you add energy and mental breaks into the schedule, you could wrap this up in about two hours.

In a couple of hours you can start enjoying the lifelong benefits of a mentally and verbally **mastered** dobodobo quarter note vocabulary.

Comparison with Rhythm Book 101

In this book there is **no notation**. There is also no extended discussion about all the rythmisation concepts, in the introduction or chapter introductions. This book is a rhythmisation only, practical talking book.

This book assumes that you are familiar with all the frequently asked questions and glossary. If you are not, kindly consult your copy of Rhythm Book 101.

Suggestions for using this book

Read this book out loud and in tempo. Start with a low metronome tempo of MM60.

Reading aloud is the best way to talk and hear the rhythm you see. These goals may be helpful to you.

Goal 1 is to have fun with this book. This is rhythm after all.

Goal 2 is to **pronounce the *vowel lengths* correctly** [e, u and o] in this book.

Goal 3 is to pronounce the *consonants* [d, b, s] in exactly the right place.

Goal 4 is to read and **talk *rhythm words*** rather than rhythm syllables.

Goal 5 is to train your lips, tongue, and jaw to **talk** the 25 **rhythm words** in this vocabulary fluently and **accurately**.

Goal 6 is to read and say a line of four rhythm words at a time.

Goal 7 is to fluently **talk** fourteen hundred and ninety-eight bars **in tempo** with your metronome set to MM60.

About Rhythmisation Levels

This primer is a rhythmisation aid for musicians *and guitar players* who do *not* read music or rhythm notation.

What is Rhythmisation? Rhythmisation is a both a process (verb) and a system (noun).

Rhythmisation is a process of communicating rhythm with written text or spoken words instead of musical notation.

Solmisation communicates musical pitch with written text or spoken words (solfa or solfeggio) instead of musical notation.

Rhythmisation is the rhythm equivalent of solmisation.

Rhythmisation is a system of rhythm *levels* and vocabularies.

The basic note names that are favoured by American music teachers, is contrasted with rhythmisation names in this table.

numeral	note	rhythmisation
1	whole note	**debedebe**
2	half note	**dubudubu**
4	quarter note	**dobodobo**
8	eighth note	**dabadaba**
16	sixteenth note	**dibidibi**

The names of the classical rhythm levels are contrasted with the rhythmisation equivalents in this table.

numeral	classical	rhythmisation
1	semibreve	**debedebe**
2	minim	**dubudubu**
4	crotchet	**dobodobo**
8	quaver	**dabadaba**
16	semiquaver	**dibidibi**

Each rhythmisation rhythm level is now explained.

Debedebe is the rhythm word for four whole notes. The vowel [e] *as pronounced* in "red" is spoken for one whole note duration. The [e] vowel is twice as long as the [u] vowel.

Dubudubu is the rhythm word for four half notes. The vowel [u] *as pronounced* in "blue" is spoken for one half note duration. The [u] vowel is twice as long as the [o] vowel.

Dobodobo is the rhythm word for four quarter notes. The vowel [o] *as pronounced* in "go" is spoken for one quarter note duration. The [o] vowel is twice as long as the [a] vowel.

Dabadaba is the rhythm word for four eighth notes. The vowel [a] *as pronounced* in "path" is spoken for one eighth note duration. The [a] vowel is twice as long as the [i] vowel.

Dibidibi is the rhythm word for four sixteenth notes. The vowel [i] *as pronounced* in "beat" is spoken for one sixteenth note duration. The [i] vowel is half as long as the [a] vowel.

The consonants [d, b. s] are pronounced as usual in English.

Rhythmisation Pronunciation Guide

Vowel Pronunciation

- [e] as in 'red'
- [u] as in 'blue'
- [o] as in 'go'
- [a] as in 'path'
- [i] as in 'beat'

Vowel Length

- [e] is twice as long as [u]
- [u] is twice as long as [o]
- [o] is twice as long as [a]
- [a] is twice as long as [i]

- [i] is half as long as [a]
- [a] is half as long as [o]
- [o] is half as long as [u]
- [u] is half as long as [e]

Dobodobo Vocabulary Vowel Lengths

- [e] lasts 4 clicks
- [uo] or [ou] lasts 3 clicks
- [u] lasts 2 clicks
- [o] lasts 1 click

Table of One Bar Rhythmisation Levels

1   de

2   du   bu

4   do   bo   do   bo

8   da ba da ba da ba da ba

16   dibidibi dibidibi dibidibi dibidibi

Table of Two Bar Rhythmisation Levels

1   de   be

2   du   bu   du   bu

4   do   bo   do   bo   do   bo   do   bo

8   da ba da ba da ba da ba da ba da ba da ba da ba

16   dibidibi dibidibi dibidibi dibidibi dibidibi dibidibi dibidibi dibidibi

Rhythm Definition 101 Quarter Note Rhythmisations Vocabulary

This is the vocabulary of twenty-five quarter note rhythmisations.

Vocabulary Table

4 Attacks	3 Attacks	2 Attacks	1 Attack	0 Attack
dobodobo	dobobu	dobou	de	se
	dobubo	dubu	be	
	dudobo	duobo	sobou	
	sobodobo	sobobu	subu	
	dobodoso	sobubo	suobo	
	dobosobo	sudobo		
	dosodobo	dobosu		
		dosodoso		
		dosubo		
		sobodoso		
		sobosobo		

Vocabulary List

The vocabulary may also be presented like this:

4 Attacks
dobodobo.

3 Attacks

dobobu, dobubo, dudobo, sobodobo, dobodoso, dobosobo, dosodobo.

2 Attacks

dobou, dubu, duobo, sobobu, sobubo, sudobo, dobosu, dosodoso, dosubo, sobodoso, sobosobo.

1 Attack

de, be, sobou, subu, suobo.

0 Attack

se.

Suggested ways to review this vocabulary

Review these rhythms over three rounds with your metronome set to MM60.

In Round 1, say each rhythm four times ensuring that each consonant you say sounds *exactly* in time with the click.

In Round 2, say each rhythm four times ensuring that each vowel you say lasts the full duration and the correct number of clicks.

In Round 3, say each rhythm four times ensuring that each consonant you say sounds *exactly* in time with the click and that each vowel you say lasts the full duration.

Rhythm Talking Section

EIGHT ATTACK RHYTHMS

8 Attack Rhythms 4+4

1   **dobodobo** dobodobo

SEVEN ATTACK RHYTHMS

7 Attack Rhythms 4+3 CV

3   **dobodobo** dobobu dobodobo dobubo

7   dobodobo dudobo dobodobo sobodobo

11   dobodobo dobosobo dobodobo dosodobo

15   dobodobo dobodoso

7 Attack Rhythms 3+4 VC

17   dobobu **dobodobo** dobubo dobodobo

21   dudobo dobodobo sobodobo dobodobo

25   dobosobo dobodobo dosodobo dobodobo

29   dobodoso dobodobo

SIX ATTACK RHYTHMS

6 Attack Rhythms 4+2 CV

31   **dobodobo** duobo dobodobo sobobu

35   dobodobo sobubo dobodobo sudobo

39   dobodobo sobosobo dobodobo dosubo

43   dobodobo dobosu

6 Attack Rhythms 3+3 CV

45   **dobobu** dobobu dobobu dobubo

49   dobobu dudobo dobobu sobodobo

53   dobobu dobosobo dobobu dosodobo

57   dobobu dobodoso

59   **dobubo** dobobu dobubo dobubo

63   dobubo dudobo dobubo sobodobo

67	dobubo dobosobo dobubo dosodobo
71	dobubo dobodoso
73	**dudobo** dobobu dudobo dobubo
77	dudobo dudobo dudobo sobodobo
81	dudobo dobosobo dudobo dosodobo
85	dudobo dobodoso
87	**sobodobo** dobobu sobodobo dobubo
91	sobodobo dudobo sobodobo sobodobo
95	sobodobo dobosobo sobodobo dosodobo
99	sobodobo dobodoso
101	**dobodoso** dobobu dobodoso dobubo
105	dobodoso dudobo dobodoso sobodobo
109	dobodoso dobosobo dobodoso dosodobo
113	dobodoso dobodoso

115	**dobosobo** dobobu dobosobo dobubo
119	dobosobo dudobo dobosobo sobodobo
123	dobosobo dobosobo dobosobo dosodobo
127	dobosobo dobodoso
129	**dosodobo** dobobu dosodobo dobubo
133	dosodobo dudobo dosodobo sobodobo
137	dosodobo dobosobo dosodobo dosodobo
141	dosodobo dobodoso

```
6 Attack Rhythms 3+3 VC
```

143	dobobu **dobobu** dobubo dobobu
147	dudobo dobobu sobodobo dobobu
151	dobosobo dobobu dosodobo dobobu
155	dobodoso dobobu
157	dobobu **dobubo** dobubo dobubo

161	dudobo dobubo sobodobo dobubo
165	dobosobo dobubo dosodobo dobubo
169	dobodoso dobubo
171	dobobu **dudobo** dobubo dudobo
175	dudobo dudobo sobodobo dudobo
179	dobosobo dudobo dosodobo dudobo
183	dobodoso dudobo
185	dobobu **sobodobo** dobubo sobodobo
189	dudobo sobodobo sobodobo sobodobo
193	dobosobo sobodobo dosodobo sobodobo
197	dobodoso sobodobo
199	dobobu **dobodoso** dobubo dobodoso
203	dudobo dobodoso sobodobo dobodoso
207	dobosobo dobodoso dosodobo dobodoso

211   dobodoso dobodoso

213   dobobu **dobosobo** dobubo dobosobo

217   dudobo dobosobo sobodobo dobosobo

221   dobosobo dobosobo dosodobo dobosobo

225   dobodoso dobosobo

227   dobobu **dosodobo** dobubo dosodobo

231   dudobo dosodobo sobodobo dosodobo

235   dobosobo dosodobo dosodobo dosodobo

239   dobodoso dosodobo

6 Attack Rhythms 2+4 VC

241   dobou **dobodobo** dubu dobodobo

245   duobo dobodobo sobobu dobodobo

249   sobubo dobodobo sudobo dobodobo

253   dobosu dobodobo dosodoso dobodobo

257   dosubo dobodobo sobodoso dobodobo

261   sobosobo dobodobo

FIVE ATTACK RHYTHMS

5 Attack Rhythms 4+1

263   **dobodobo** be

5 Attack Rhythms 3+2 VC

265   **dobobu** dobou dobobu dubu

269   dobobu duobo dobobu sobobu

273   dobobu sobubo dobobu sudobo

277   dobobu dobosu dobobu dosodoso

281   dobobu dosubo dobobu sobodoso

285   dobobu sobosobo

287   **dobubo** dobou dobubo dubu

291   dobubo duobo dobubo sobobu

295   dobubo sobubo dobubo sudobo

299   dobubo dobosu dobubo dosodoso

303   dobubo dosubo dobubo sobodoso

307   dobubo sobosobo

309   **dudobo** dobou dudobo dubu

313   dudobo duobo dudobo sobobu

317   dudobo sobubo dudobo sudobo

321   dudobo dobosu dudobo dosodoso

325   dudobo dosubo dudobo sobodoso

329   dudobo sobosobo

331   **sobodobo** dobou sobodobo dubu

335   sobodobo duobo sobodobo sobobu

339   sobodobo sobubo sobodobo sudobo

343   sobodobo dobosu sobodobo dosodoso

347   sobodobo dosubo sobodobo sobodoso

351   sobodobo sobosobo

353   **dobodoso** dobou dobodoso dubu

357   dobodoso duobo dobodoso sobobu

361   dobodoso sobubo dobodoso sudobo

365   dobodoso dobosu dobodoso dosodoso

369   dobodoso dosubo dobodoso sobodoso

373   dobodoso sobosobo

375   **dobosobo** dobou dobosobo dubu

379   dobosobo duobo dobosobo sobobu

383   dobosobo sobubo dobosobo sudobo

387   dobosobo dobosu dobosobo dosodoso

391   dobosobo dosubo dobosobo sobodoso

395   dobosobo sobosobo

397   **dosodobo** dobou dosodobo dubu

401   dosodobo duobo dosodobo sobobu

405   dosodobo sobubo dosodobo sudobo

409   dosodobo dobosu dosodobo dosodoso

413   dosodobo dosubo dosodobo sobodoso

417   dosodobo sobosobo

5 Attack Rhythms 2+3 CV

419   **dobou** dobobu dobou dobubo

423   dobou dudobo dobou sobodobo

427   dobou dobosobo dobou dosodobo

431   dobou dobodoso

433   **dubu** dobobu dubu dobubo

437   dubu dudobo dubu sobodobo

441   dubu dobosobo dubu dosodobo

445   dubu dobodoso

447   **duobo** dobobu duobo dobubo

451   duobo dudobo duobo sobodobo

455   duobo dobosobo duobo dosodobo

459   duobo dobodoso

461   **sobobu** dobobu sobobu dobubo

465   sobobu dudobo sobobu sobodobo

469   sobobu dobosobo sobobu dosodobo

473   sobobu dobodoso

475   **sudobo** dobobu sudobo dobubo

479   sudobo dudobo sudobo sobodobo

483   sudobo dobosobo sudobo dosodobo

487   sudobo dobodoso

489   **dobosu** dobobu dobosu dobubo

493   dobosu dudobo dobosu sobodobo

497   dobosu dobosobo dobosu dosodobo

501   dobosu dobodoso

503   **dosodoso** dobobu dosodoso dobubo

507   dosodoso dudobo dosodoso sobodobo

511   dosodoso dobosobo dosodoso dosodobo

515   dosodoso dobodoso

517   **dosubo** dobobu dosubo dobubo

521   dosubo dudobo dosubo sobodobo

525   dosubo dobosobo dosubo dosodobo

529   dosubo dobodoso

531   **sobodoso** dobobu sobodoso dobubo

535   sobodoso dudobo sobodoso sobodobo

539   sobodoso dobosobo sobodoso dosodobo

543   sobodoso dobodoso

545   **sobosobo** dobobu sobosobo dobubo

549   sobosobo dudobo sobosobo sobodobo

553   sobosobo dobosobo sobosobo dosodobo

557   sobosobo dobodoso

5 Attack Rhythms 1+4

559   **de** dobodobo

FOUR ATTACK RHYTHMS

4 Attack Rhythms 4+0

561 **dobodobo** se

4 Attack Rhythms 3+1 CV

563 **dobobu** be dobobu sobou

567 dobobu subu dobobu suobo

571 **dobubo** be dobubo sobou

575 dobubo subu dobubo suobo

579 **dudobo** be dudobo sobou

583 dudobo subu dudobo suobo

587 **sobodobo** be sobodobo sobou

591 sobodobo subu sobodobo suobo

595   **dobodoso** be dobodoso sobou

599   dobodoso subu dobodoso suobo

603   **dobosobo** be dobosobo sobou

607   dobosobo subu dobosobo suobo

611   **dosodobo** be dosodobo sobou

615   dosodobo subu dosodobo suobo

4 Attack Rhythms 2+2 CV

619   **dobou** dobou dobou dubu

623   dobou duobo dobou sobobu

627   dobou sobubo dobou sudobo

631   dobou dobosu dobou dosodoso

635   dobou dosubo dobou sobodoso

639   dobou sobosobo

641   **dubu** dobou dubu dubu

645	dubu duobo dubu sobobu
649	dubu sobubo dubu sudobo
653	dubu dobosu dubu dosodoso
657	dubu dosubo dubu sobodoso
661	dubu sobosobo
663	**duobo** dobou duobo dubu
667	duobo duobo duobo sobobu
671	duobo sobubo duobo sudobo
675	duobo dobosu duobo dosodoso
679	duobo dosubo duobo sobodoso
683	duobo sobosobo
685	**sobobu** dobou sobobu dubu
689	sobobu duobo sobobu sobobu

693   sobobu sobubo sobobu sudobo

697   sobobu dobosu sobobu dosodoso

701   sobobu dosubo sobobu sobodoso

705   sobobu sobosobo

707   **sobubo** dobou sobubo dubu

711   sobubo duobo sobubo sobobu

715   sobubo sobubo sobubo sudobo

719   sobubo dobosu sobubo dosodoso

723   sobubo dosubo sobubo sobodoso

727   sobubo sobosobo

729   **sudobo** dobou sudobo dubu

733   sudobo duobo sudobo sobobu

737   sudobo sobubo sudobo sudobo

741   sudobo dobosu sudobo dosodoso

745   sudobo dosubo sudobo sobodoso

749   sudobo sobosobo

751   **dobosu** dobou dobosu dubu

755   dobosu duobo dobosu sobobu

759   dobosu sobubo dobosu sudobo

763   dobosu dobosu dobosu dosodoso

767   dobosu dosubo dobosu sobodoso

771   dobosu sobosobo

773   **dosodoso** dobou dosodoso dubu

777   dosodoso duobo dosodoso sobobu

781   dosodoso sobubo dosodoso sudobo

785   dosodoso dobosu dosodoso dosodoso

789   dosodoso dosubo dosodoso sobodoso

793   dosodoso sobosobo

795   **dosubo** dobou dosubo dubu

799   dosubo duobo dosubo sobobu

803   dosubo sobubo dosubo sudobo

807   dosubo dobosu dosubo dosodoso

811   dosubo dosubo dosubo sobodoso

815   dosubo sobosobo

817   **sobodoso** dobou sobodoso dubu

821   sobodoso duobo sobodoso sobobu

825   sobodoso sobubo sobodoso sudobo

829   sobodoso dobosu sobodoso dosodoso

833   sobodoso dosubo sobodoso sobodoso

837   sobodoso sobosobo

839   **sobosobo** dobou sobosobo dubu

843   sobosobo duobo sobosobo sobobu

847   sobosobo sobubo sobosobo sudobo

851   sobosobo dobosu sobosobo dosodoso

855   sobosobo dosubo sobosobo sobodoso

859   sobosobo sobosobo

4 Attack Rhythms 2+2 VC

861   dobou **dobou** dubu dobou

865   duobo dobou sobobu dobou

869   sobubo dobou sudobo dobou

873   dobosu dobou dosodoso dobou

877   dosubo dobou sobodoso dobou

881   sobosobo dobou

883   dobou **dubu** dubu dubu

887   duobo dubu sobobu dubu

891   sobubo dubu sudobo dubu

895   dobosu dubu dosodoso dubu

899   dosubo dubu sobodoso dubu

903   sobosobo dubu

905   dobou **duobo** dubu duobo

909   duobo duobo sobobu duobo

913   sobubo duobo sudobo duobo

917   dobosu duobo dosodoso duobo

921   dosubo duobo sobodoso duobo

925   sobosobo duobo

927   dobou **sobobu** dubu sobobu

931   duobo sobobu sobobu sobobu

935	sobubo sobobu sudobo sobobu
939	dobosu sobobu dosodoso sobobu
943	dosubo sobobu sobodoso sobobu
947	sobosobo sobobu
949	dobou **sobubo** dubu sobubo
953	duobo sobubo sobobu sobubo
957	sobubo sobubo sudobo sobubo
961	dobosu sobubo dosodoso sobubo
965	dosubo sobubo sobodoso sobubo
969	sobosobo sobubo
971	dobou **sudobo** dubu sudobo
975	duobo sudobo sobobu sudobo
979	sobubo sudobo sudobo sudobo

983   dobosu sudobo dosodoso sudobo

987   dosubo sudobo sobodoso sudobo

991   sobosobo sudobo

993   dobou **dobosu** dubu dobosu

997   duobo dobosu sobobu dobosu

1001 sobubo dobosu sudobo dobosu

1005 dobosu dobosu dosodoso dobosu

1009 dosubo dobosu sobodoso dobosu

1013 sobosobo dobosu

1015 dobou **dosodoso** dubu dosodoso

1019 duobo dosodoso sobobu dosodoso

1023 sobubo dosodoso sudobo dosodoso

1027 dobosu dosodoso dosodoso dosodoso

1031 dosubo dosodoso sobodoso dosodoso

1035   sobosobo dosodoso

1037   dobou **dosubo** dubu dosubo

1041   duobo dosubo sobobu dosubo

1045   sobubo dosubo sudobo dosubo

1049   dobosu dosubo dosodoso dosubo

1053   dosubo dosubo sobodoso dosubo

1057   sobosobo dosubo

1059   dobou **sobodoso** dubu sobodoso

1063   duobo sobodoso sobobu sobodoso

1067   sobubo sobodoso sudobo sobodoso

1071   dobosu sobodoso dosodoso sobodoso

1075   dosubo sobodoso sobodoso sobodoso

1079   sobosobo sobodoso

1081   dobou **sobosobo** dubu sobosobo

1085   duobo sobosobo sobobu sobosobo

1089   sobubo sobosobo sudobo sobosobo

1093   dobosu sobosobo dosodoso sobosobo

1097   dosubo sobosobo sobodoso sobosobo

1101   sobosobo sobosobo

4 Attack Rhythms 1+3 VC

1113   de **dobobu** sobou dobobu

1117   subu dobobu suobo dobobu

1121   de **dobubo** sobou dobubo

1125   subu dobubo suobo dobubo

1129   de **dudobo** sobou dudobo

1133   subu dudobo suobo dudobo

1137	de **sobodobo** sobou sobodobo
1141	subu sobodobo suobo sobodobo
1145	de **dobodoso** sobou dobodoso
1149	subu dobodoso suobo dobodoso
1153	de **dobosobo** sobou dobosobo
1157	subu dobosobo suobo dobosobo
1161	de **dosodobo** sobou dosodobo
1165	subu dosodobo suobo dosodobo

4 Attack Rhythms 0+4

1169   **se** dobodobo

THREE ATTACK RHYTHMS

3 Attack Rhythms 3+0 VC

1171   dobobu **se** dobubo se

1175   dudobo se sobodobo se

1179   dobodoso se dobosobo se

1183   dosodobo se

3 Attack Rhythms 2+1 VC

1185   dobou **be** dubu be

1189   duobo be sobobu be

1193   sobubo be sudobo be

1197   dobosu be dosodoso be

1201   dosubo be sobodoso be

1205   sobosobo be

1207	dobou **sobou** dubu sobou
1211	duobo sobou sobobu sobou
1215	sobubo sobou sudobo sobou
1219	dobosu sobou dosodoso sobou
1223	dosubo sobou sobodoso sobou
1227	sobosobo sobou
1229	dobou **subu** dubu subu
1233	duobo subu sobobu subu
1237	sobubo subu sudobo subu
1241	dobosu subu dosodoso subu
1245	dosubo subu sobodoso subu
1249	sobosobo subu
1251	dobou **suobo** dubu suobo
1255	duobo suobo sobobu suobo

```
1259      sobubo suobo sudobo suobo

1263      dobosu suobo dosodoso suobo

1267      dosubo suobo sobodoso suobo

1271      sobosobo suobo

          3 Attack Rhythms 1+2 CV

1273      **de** dobou de dubu

1277      de duobo de sobobu

1281      de sobubo de sudobo

1285      de dobosu de dosodoso

1289      de dosubo de sobodoso

1293      de sobosobo

1295      **sobou** dobou sobou dubu

1299      sobou duobo sobou sobobu

1303      sobou sobubo sobou sudobo
```

1307   sobou dobosu sobou dosodoso

1311   sobou dosubo sobou sobodoso

1315   sobou sobosobo

1317   **subu** dobou subu dubu

1321   subu duobo subu sobobu

1325   subu sobubo subu sudobo

1329   subu dobosu subu dosodoso

1333   subu dosubo subu sobodoso

1337   subu sobosobo

1339   **suobo** dobou suobo dubu

1343   suobo duobo suobo sobobu

1347   suobo sobubo suobo sudobo

1351   suobo dobosu suobo dosodoso

1355   suobo dosubo suobo sobodoso

1359   suobo sobosobo

3 Attack Rhythms 0+3 CV

1361   **se** dobobu se dobubo

1365   se dudobo se sobodobo

1369   se dobodoso se dobosobo

1373   se dosodobo

TWO ATTACK RHYTHMS

2 Attack Rhythms 2+0 VC

1375   dobou **se** dubu se

1379   duobo se sobobu se

1383   sobubo se sudobo se

1387   dobosu se dosodoso se

1391   dosubo se sobodoso se

1395   sobosobo se

2 Attack Rhythms 1+1 CV

1397   **de** be de sobou

1401   de subu de suobo

1405   **sobou** be sobou sobou

1409   sobou subu sobou suobo

1413   **subu** be subu sobou

1417   subu subu subu suobo

1421   **suobo** be suobo sobou

1425   suobo subu suobo suobo

2 Attack Rhythms 1+1 VC

1429   de **be** sobou be

1433   subu be suobo be

1437   de **sobou** sobou sobou

1441   subu sobou suobo sobou

1445   de **subu** sobou subu

1449   subu subu suobo subu

1453   de **suobo** sobou suobo

1457   subu suobo suobo suobo

2 Attack Rhythms 0+2 CV

1461   **se** dobou se dubu

1465   se duobo se sobobu

1469   se sobubo se sudobo

1473   se dobosu se dosodoso

1477   se dosubo se sobodoso

1481   se sobosobo

ONE ATTACK RHYTHMS

1 Attack Rhythms 1+0 VC

1483 de **se** sobou se

1487 subu se suobo se

1 Attack Rhythms 0+1

1491 **se** be se sobou CV

1495 se subu se suobo

NO ATTACK RHYTHMS

0 Attack Rhythms 0+0

1497 **Se** se

Congratulations

Congratulations! You have taken a huge step forward with your dobodobo quarter rhythm skills.

You have continued your dobodobo rhythm mastery that you started with Rhythm Book 101.

You have extended your verbal command of the dobodobo vocabulary with simple English text instructions only.

You have verbally mastered three different vowel durations: e, u, and o as separate vowels and as diphthongs across a twenty-five word vocabulary and fourteen hundred and ninety-eight bars. Good going!

You have practiced talking dobodobo's in time with your metronome.

The biggest thing that you have done--that you may not properly appreciate yet because these skills are still very recent additions to your motor system--is that you have set up your dobodobo head. Without your dobodobo head, your confident dobodobo rhythm arm and tempo leg is not possible.

Out of all the vocabularies, dobodobo is the most important one to master verbally. Because it is the foundation vocabulary.

Dobodobo is the one vocabulary that divides into the dabadaba (8th note) vocabulary, and subdivides into the dibidibi (16th note) vocabulary.

Dobodobo is also the vocabulary that doubles into the dubudubu (half note) vocabulary and quadruples into the debedebe (whole note) vocabulary.

By experiencing all fourteen hundred and ninety-eight bars in this book you have experienced the *pivotal* rhythm vocabulary of them all. Congratulations!

Musically, you now know how to deal with single line rhythm. This is the horizontal essence of playing music on your instrument.

And you have also built up enough rhythmisation experience to take advantage of some hidden benefits. One is your ability to write down, in notation, any dobodobo rhythm you can say and play. This is the hidden benefit of transcription. You will find that you can *actually* transcribe any dobodobo rhythm you can talk and play.

Thank you for making Rhythm Definition 101 Quarter Note Rhythms Examples, Exercises and Patterns part of your rhythm skill and artistry base.

Where to next?

I recommend you go through the Rhythm Guitar 101 Quarter Note Strumming Patterns next.

You will extend your **head** command of dobodobo rhythms to your **strumming arm** and **tempo foot** command. This means you will be physiologically embedding the dobodobo vocabulary and conversations into your strumming arm so that when you *brain thinks* a rhythm, your *arm strums* the rhythm automatically, in time with the tempo in your feet.

Appendices

How Long To Read This Book

This table shows you how long it will take to talk fourteen hundred and ninety eight bars in tempo at the following tempos. This time is talking time only. You will need to add in energy and mental break times on top.

mm	hrs	mins
60	1	40
64	1	34
68	1	28
72	1	23
76	1	19
80	1	15
84	1	11
88	1	8
92	1	5
96	1	2
100	1	0
104		58
108		55
112		54
116		52
120		50
124		48
128		47
132		45
136		44

About the Author

I am Taura Eruera and I live in Grey Lynn, Auckland, New Zealand. Apart from a decade off in the 90's I have taught guitar continuously since 1982. That experience included teaching harmony, rhythm and guitar at the School of Creative Musicianship for six years followed by private teaching, seminars and clinics.

Over the years I have written many titles for guitar, melody, harmony and rhythm instruction. My titles have been self-published for in-house and private student consumption or for publication on self-owned websites. Over this time my energy has been focused more on creation than distribution. Now with platforms like Amazon Kindle available, I am formatting my catalogue of work for wider distribution.

Much of my writing has come out of my studies with Dick Grove, Howard Roberts and, more importantly, directly out of my teaching experience. I am grateful to a crazy diamond of a guitar player named Clash for being my pioneer rhythmisation dabadaba student, way back in the day. Clash reckoned that his skill in verbalising the Dabadaba's enabled him to put his strumming and picking hand on auto pilot, which made life that much easier for him at the Guitar Institute of Technology.

Guitar teaching has been a major activity for me over the years. Teaching has always alternated with gigging and other activities in my work life: old school, session work before the computer; transcription and lead sheet preparation and digital session work after computers came in.

Activities outside guitar teaching extended to business consultation, business start ups, founding roles in radio and health care companies, software development and search engine optimization services.

Even though I am involved in many interests, guitar teaching remains an important part of my week. Writing up those insights remains an important part of my teaching.

Join Rhythmisation Insights

Thank you for reading this book. I hope you find this book useful and thorough. Let me invite you to join the Rhythmisation Insights Group.

Simply paste this URL into your web browser --
https://tinyurl.com/dobodobo101

You will be redirected to a page where you can enter your details in the sign up form and join the discoveries!

Expect lots of useful information that we just couldn't include in this book. Expect real life resources from real people, like you, sharing their experiences and insights with you. Expect a lot of your questions to be discussed, shared and answered. Want to know a reader's tip for how to read this book on a music stand? See you on the inside.

Kind regards,
Taura

Learn more about Rhythmisation

Facebook Rhythmisation Group

https://www.facebook.com/rhythmisation

Rhythm Books and Rhythm Patterns

https://www.pinterest.com/rhythmisation/rhythm-books-and-rhythm-patterns/

Linked In Rhythm Teachers and Students

https://www.linkedin.com/grp/home?gid=8341686

Rhythmisation Google+

https://plus.google.com/102949469753221832406/posts

Twitter

https://twitter.com/rhythmisation

Rhythmisation on Youtube

https://www.youtube.com/channel/UCtjqcKig1Tg7h7PTiT4lOwg

Rhythmisation

http://www.rhythmisation.com

Rhythmisation Music School

http://rhythmisationmusicschool.viewcy.com/

Rhythm Definition 101 Quarter Note Video Course

http://taura.evsuite.com/rhythm-definition-101-video-course-optin/

www.ingramcontent.com/pod-product-compliance
Lightning Source LLC
Chambersburg PA
CBHW061340040426
42444CB00011B/3015